THE HUNDRED YEARS' WAR

A Century of War Between England and France

Written by Marie Fauré
In collaboration with Benoît-J. Pédretti
Translated by Rebecca Neal

History 50MINUTES.com

THE HUNDRED YEARS' WAR

KEY INFORMATION

- **When:** 1337-1453.
- **Where:** France.
- **Context:** the King of France died without a direct heir, leaving the throne vacant. There followed a series of conflicts over the space of around a hundred years which pitted England against France in order to obtain political and economic domination over Western Europe.
- **Countries involved:** France versus England.
- **Key protagonists:**
  - Edward III, King of England and Duke of Aquitaine (1312-1377).
  - Bertrand du Guesclin, constable of France (c. 1320-1380).
  - Charles VII, King of France (1403-1461).
- **Outcome:** French victory.
- **Victims:** the number of victims, both direct and indirect, is difficult to estimate.

INTRODUCTION

The Hundred Years' War is one of the most famous conflicts of the Middle Ages and one of the longest direct clashes between two major powers. Between 1337 and 1453, it set the two most important monarchies of the Medieval West, France and England, against one another. When the King of England Edward III claimed his right to the French throne in 1337, he stepped right into the dynastic conflicts between the House of Plantagenet and the House of Valois. However, the real aim of the conflict proved much more important than that: it involved nothing more or less than obtaining political and economic domination over Western Europe. More than a century later, when the English were defeated at the Battle of Castillon in 1453, this rivalry had turned into a full-scale war between the two nations. Nonetheless, their armies had not fought without interruption for 116 years, as battles were interspersed with many periods of truce.

Although the previous centuries had been prosperous, misfortunes seemed to overwhelm the medieval world in the early 14th century. In 1347, the Black Death and famine decimated the population, as did the many campaigns which took place during the Hundred Years' War, which proved to be particularly deadly and devastating.

At first glance, the forces of the countries at war do not seem to be evenly matched. France was enjoying great economic, cultural and demographic standing (it had 15 million inhabitants at the start of the century), while England had a lower population (under 5 million inhabitants) and was already embroiled in a war with Scotland. Even so, it was England that had the advantage between 1337 and 1360. France then reconquered its territories until 1415, when England regained the upper hand. The arrival of Joan of Arc (French heroine, 1412-1431), the alliance with Burgundy and the reform of the army finally gave the advantage to France, which won the war in 1453. The English then had no territory left on the continent, apart from Calais.

The Hundred Years' War was of vital importance on a number of levels. It brought the European monarchies into the age of modernity and gave rise to a national feeling that did not exist before, thus marking a turning point in the history and development of Europe.

CONTEXT

THE ENGLISH KING AS A VASSAL OF THE FRENCH KING

The bonds linking the kingdoms of France and England date back to the 11th century. In 1066, William the Conqueror (c. 1028-1087) seized power in England at the Battle of Hastings, in this way connecting the destinies of the two countries.

It was not until the next century that one of the main causes of tension between the two countries emerged: the seizure of the Duchy of Aquitaine by the English kings. In 1137, Eleanor of Aquitaine, Duchess of Aquitaine and Countess of Poitiers (c. 1122-1204), married King Louis VII of France (1120-1180). However, relations between the couple quickly deteriorated and Louis the Younger, as much to save his honour as to remedy the lack of a male heir, sought an annulment on the grounds that the couple were too closely related in the eyes of the Church. A few months later, Eleanor married Henry Plantagenet (1133-1189), the heir to the English throne. She became queen of England in 1154. The Duchy of Aquitaine, which belonged to her, therefore escaped French domination. From then on, the French kings tried to recover the territories under Plantagenet control by any means possible. King Philip II of France (1165-1223) managed to recover the majority of these lands through arms and diplomacy, with the exception of Guyenne (a variant of Aquitaine). It was not until 1259 that the Treaty of Paris between King Louis IX of France (1214-1270) and King

Henry III of England (1207-1272) temporarily resolved the status of the duchy. Although Henry III kept the title Duke of Aquitaine, in return he had to pay homage to the king of France. Immediately prior to the Hundred Years' War, the situation was therefore particularly ambiguous: the king of England was both sovereign of his kingdom and vassal of the king of France because of Aquitaine, which he found difficult to accept.

This submissive relationship to the new king of France, Philip VI (1293-1350) was especially difficult for Edward III to accept because Philip was only the son of a count, whereas he was the son of a king.

A VACANT THRONE

It was in this context that an unprecedented event occurred for the Capet dynasty, which had been in power in France for over three centuries: King Charles IV, called the Fair (c. 1295-

1328), the last son of Philip IV, also called the Fair (1268-1314), died in 1328 without leaving a male heir. Consequently, the leading figures of the country had to choose between two claimants: Philip of Valois (1293-1350), the first cousin of the late king, and Edward III, the grandson of Philip the Fair on his mother's side, the nephew of the late king and king of England. The French, who were reluctant to bring together the two crowns in favour of the English, decided to recognise Philip of Valois as king of France. He was crowned and took the name Philip VI. They justified this choice through Salic law, which excluded women from the line of succession and the transmission of power. Edward III, preoccupied with various matters in Scotland, did not contest this decision and even paid homage to the new king in 1329 on behalf of Aquitaine, as a mere duke.

SALIC LAW

Salic law was officially presented by the theorists of this time as a law inherited from the Salian Franks, a people who had lived during the 5th century. In reality, it was entirely invented in 1316 to remove Joan (1311-1349), the daughter of Louis X (1289-1316), from the line of succession. Joan's legitimacy was contested following accusations of adultery against her mother. From this date onwards, women were officially excluded from power in the kingdom of France. In 1328, the law was modified so as to also exclude women from the right to the throne. Isabella of France (c. 1292-1358), the mother of Edward III, therefore could not inherit the crown or pass it on to her descendants.

From 1332-1333, there was an increasing number of reasons for disagreement. The King of France supported the Scottish rebellion against the English, in this way complying with a series of treaties signed in the previous century. Furthermore, the unrest in Flanders, which had been placed under the protection of France through homage, put the alliances between the two kingdoms to the test. Edward III supported the revolt of the cloth-making towns and decreed an embargo on wool, which seriously weakened the territory's economy. Finally, when Philip VI raised a fleet to go on a crusade in 1335, England felt threatened with invasion and formed a coalition against France. In response, the King seized the Duchy of Aquitaine on 24 May 1337. Edward III reacted by claiming his right to the French crown. As such, on 1 November 1337, he sent the Bishop of Lincoln to Paris bearing letters in which he addressed the French King merely as "Philip de Valois" and claimed that the French throne was not rightfully his (Sumption, 1990: 232). Following this slight on the King's honour, war was declared.

Beyond the dynastic quarrel and Edward III's desire to no longer have to pay homage to the king of France, the issues of the two kingdoms were primarily economic and strategic. From Flanders to Aquitaine, the two sides both wanted control of the sea ports and the richest regions in Europe. Flanders and Hainaut remained the foremost ports for the exportation of English wool, and their alliance with England was further strengthened by Edward III's marriage to Philippa of Hainaut (1314-1369) in 1328. Meanwhile, Aquitaine, which offered access to the Atlantic, was crucial to the wine trade. Furthermore, it had provided English troops with support and a base on the continent for three centuries.

The succession crisis in France - Genealogical chart

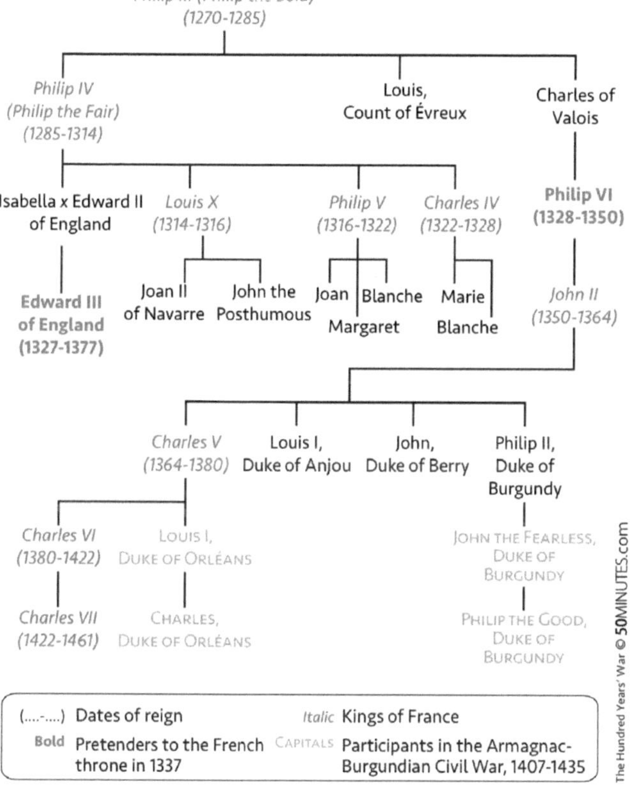

KEY PROTAGONISTS

EDWARD III, KING OF ENGLAND AND DUKE OF AQUITAINE

The son of the King of England Edward II and Isabella of France, from a very early age Edward III was a pawn in his parents' struggle for power. In 1325, at the age of just 13, he received the titles of Duke of Aquitaine and Count of Ponthieu, for which he had to pay homage to King Charles IV of France. In 1328, his mother proclaimed him king of England, thus forcing his father to abdicate.

His 50-year reign was marked by wars and political crises. His first military operation, against Scotland in the summer of 1327, ended with forced negotiations with Robert the Bruce (King of Scotland, 1274-1329). While clashes continued, Edward III increasingly focused on French affairs. The mounting tensions between Edward III and the King of France Philip IV, mainly linked to English possessions on the continent, led to the outbreak of what would become known as the Hundred Years' War. In January 1340, Edward III took the title and the coat of arms of the king of France.

Although he initially won a string of victories thanks to the strategy known as the chevauchée and the use of very mobile troops, the royal coffers gradually emptied, leading to several serious political crises during his reign. During periods of truce, Edward III reorganised his kingdom with regard to justice, currency, taxes and finance. He also developed the woollen industry in order to make France less dependent on Flanders. In addition, his resounding victories on French soil gave him the opportunity to promote the chivalric ideal by creating the Most Noble Order of the Garter in 1348, in celebration of the victories in Crécy (1346) and Calais (1347).

The Battle of Crécy, illustration from the *Chronicles* of Jean Froissart, 15th century.

A few years later, with his health worsening, he was forced to keep out of the affairs of the kingdom. He died on 21 June 1377, when the country was in the midst of a new parliamentary crisis. Beloved by the people, Edward III was remembered as a king with remarkable skills as a soldier and commander, which would be praised by his successors.

BERTRAND DU GUESCLIN, CONSTABLE OF FRANCE

The eldest son in a family of the lower nobility in Brittany, Bertrand du Guesclin won his spurs starting in 1341 alongside Charles, Duke of Brittany (1319-1364) in the Breton War of Succession. During the siege of Rennes (October 1356-July 1357), he was made a knight. A few months later, in December 1357, he entered the service of the dauphin of France, the future Charles V (1338-1380).

Starting in 1360, he dedicated himself to ridding French territory of free companies, bands of mercenaries who had been left with no employer at the end of the combat and who were laying waste to the country. He led them to Castile, where two claimants, Henry of Trastámara and Peter the Cruel, were fighting for the throne. He was taken prisoner during the Battle of Najéra by the heir to the English throne, Edward the Black Prince (Prince of Wales and Aquitaine, 1330-1376), the son of Edward III.

Following the final victory of Henry of Trastámara in 1369, and when hostilities were resuming in France, du Guesclin was appointed Constable of France by Charles V. He quickly became one of the most active military leaders in the French conquest of the 1370s. He died during the siege of Châteauneuf-de-Randon, on 13 July 1380, and was buried in the necropolis of the Basilica of Saint Denis on the King's orders.

Death of Bertrand du Guesclin at the Siege of Randon, illustration in a manuscript by Jean de Wavrin, 15th century.

Du Guesclin was already famous during his lifetime, and became a legendary figure shortly after his death. As skilful, loyal and courageous as he was brutal and merciless, he embodied resistance to the English enemy for the French. In 1407, he became the patron hero of the Armagnac party, then a national hero alongside Joan of Arc.

CHARLES VII, KING OF FRANCE

The youngest son of Charles VI (1368-1422) and Isabeau of Bavaria (c. 1371-1435), Charles became dauphin of the kingdom of France in 1417, following the deaths of his two elder brothers. One year later, when Paris was captured by the Burgundians, he fled with the Armagnacs and took refuge at Bourges. From there, he proclaimed himself regent of the kingdom, as his father had been suffering from bouts of insanity since 1392. Indirectly responsible for the assassination of John the Fearless, Duke of Burgundy (1371-1419), he was removed from the line of succession by the Treaty of Troyes in 1420. He then endeavoured to organise his government from his appanage in Berry and took the title of king when his father died in 1422, which resulted in the derisive nickname 'The King of Bourges'.

With the help of a young peasant girl from Lorraine named Joan of Arc, he managed to reconquer the Loire Valley. He was then taken to Reims to be crowned king of France in accordance with tradition on 17 July 1429. From then on, his position became stronger. He signed the Treaty of Arras in 1435, which ensured the neutrality of the Duke of Burgundy, and managed to reunify the kingdom and then retake Paris the following year. After his victory at the Battle of Castillon in 1453, which earned him the nickname the Victorious, he drove the English from the continent, although they retained the British bastion of Calais. Charles VII also made the most of the years of truce to completely reorganise the army and strengthen the French tax system.

Joan of Arc in Reims During the Coronation of Charles VII,
painting by Jules Eugène Lenepveu, 1886.

The end of his reign was marked by the assertion of royal authority at the expense of the great nobles and by the beginnings of economic recovery. He died in 1461 in unclear circumstances, with some details suggesting that he could have been poisoned by his son, the dauphin Louis. Although he enjoyed a certain prestige across Europe after his death, he did not leave the image of a victorious, knightly king in his subjects' minds, as he remained in the shadow of national heroes such as Joan of Arc.

THE HUNDRED YEARS' WAR

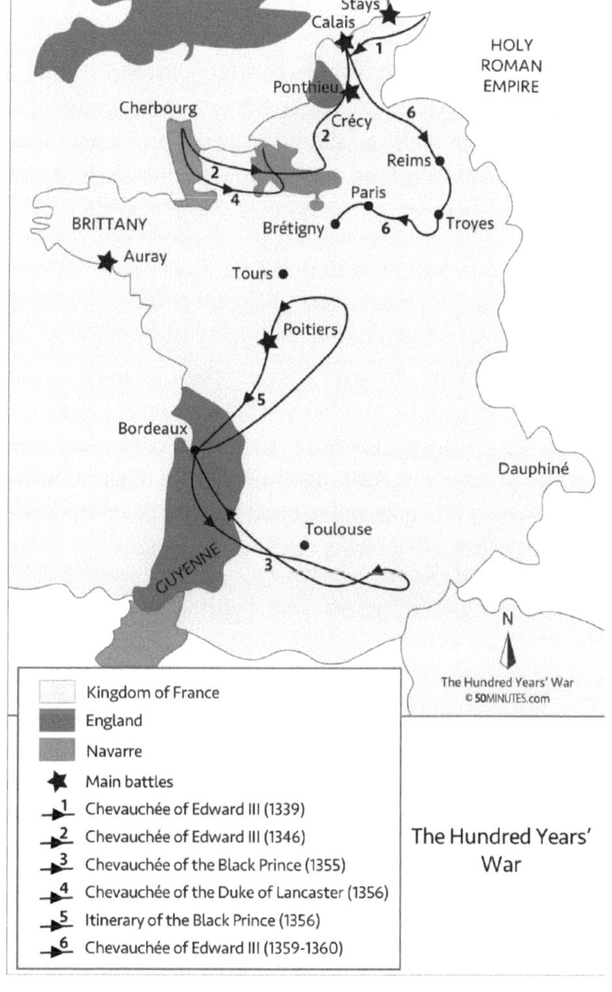

The Hundred Years' War

OVERWHELMING ENGLISH DOMINATION

The early stages of the war (1337-1340)

Although war was officially declared in 1337, the first battles did not take place until several years later. Indeed, it was not in Philip VI's interests to attack Edward III on English soil, and Edward was beset by serious financial problems caused by the war with Scotland and the many alliances he had to maintain.

It was not until 24 June 1340 that hostilities began, with the Battle of Sluys, a naval battle which took place in front of the outer port of Bruges, in Flanders. The French army's lack of experience in naval battles, the low participation of the nobility, and a number of strategic errors made this first battle a disaster for the French side, which lost three quarters of its ships. Although he had won, Edward III was forced to return to England to quell popular discontent with regard to debts, which were continually rising.

The following year, there was fighting in Brittany. As John III (Duke of Brittany, 1268-1341) had just died without leaving an heir, a war of succession broke out between his niece, Joan of Penthièvre (1319-1384), the wife of Philip VI's nephew Charles of Blois, and John of Montfort (1295-1345), the half-brother of the dead king, who was allied with the English. Edward III supported John of Montfort, seeing this dispute as an opportunity to increase his control over the Atlantic edge of Europe.

Differing military organisation

In the mid-14th century, the two adversaries had different troops at their disposal and different military strategies. The French army initially remained attached to the traditions of service and the pre-eminence of the knighthood. To form an army, there were several methods of recruitment. Firstly, there was the service that the vassals owed to their lord, amounting to 40 days over the year, with any extension of service entailing financial compensation. In addition to this, there was the arrière-ban, which summoned all free men between the aged of 18 and 60, as well as urban militias, into service. Finally, the King also called on mercenaries, mainly Genoese crossbowmen and Scottish soldiers. In this way, Philip VI managed to raise an army of 50 000 men in a few weeks, but the cost of this mobilisation did not allow him to maintain all of these men for more than four months per year. This strength in numbers was greatly reduced by a lack of flexibility in the French ranks, and by the clear contempt of the majority of nobles for the foot soldiers.

On the English side, Edward III had been able to learn from the war with Scotland and only very rarely appealed to feudal levies. He favoured a paid army, thanks to a system of contracts which linked the king to his captains and the captains to their soldiers. Although the English army never had more than 10 000 men, they proved particularly mobile and effective. This was why Edward III favoured the tactic of the chevauchée. In the course of these operations, the king or one of his sons would land in Normandy or Aquitaine, which at that time were under their control, with several thousand soldiers. From there, they crossed the kingdom of

France, taking the towns and castles that they passed and piling up their spoils in wagons to take them to Bordeaux or another bridgehead established on the continent. These operations generally only lasted for a few months and took place in summer or autumn. While some of them were successful, others ended in painful defeats, due in particular to a lack of supplies, the spread of epidemics or the excessive weight of the convoys.

The time of the great chevauchées (1345-1347)

After re-establishing order in his kingdom, in 1345 Edward III sent his armies to the continent, dividing them across three fronts: one in Brittany, one in Flanders and the other in Gascony. He landed in Normandy in July 1346 and led a major chevauchée to the north.

Although the English army tried not to fight pitched battles, which often proved very deadly, they were sometimes unavoidable. In this way, the French and English armies met at Crécy on 26 August 1346. Although it was customary for the archers and crossbowmen to open the fighting before the cavalry charge, the French horsemen decided to directly attack their enemy in order to prove their bravery and their superiority over the soldiers drawn from the common people, with no qualms about crushing their own foot soldiers. The English archers wreaked havoc with their longbows, which had a range of almost 250 metres. In the course of the battle, over 1500 men from the French cavalry, including the King's brother, were killed. This was also the first time that there were cannons on the battlefield during a pitched battle, but at this time they served more as a deterrent.

The Battle of Crécy, an illustration in *Les Grandes Chroniques de France*, around 1415.

After emerging victorious from the battle, Edward III continued his chevauchée and laid siege to Calais on 4 September 1346. As Philip VI did not come to their aid, the people of Calais surrendered on 3 August 1347. The town's inhabitants were driven out, and it would remain an advanced English bastion on the continent until 1558.

At the same time as its successes in Normandy, England's allies triumphed in Brittany, where Charles of Blois was captured, while Scotland suffered a major defeat in the north of England in 1346. However, Edward III could not take advantage of these successes because of the arrival of one of the most devastating epidemics in Western history: the Black Death.

The Battle of Poitiers and the capture of the King of France (1355-1360)

Hostilities resumed in 1355 with a chevauchée led by Edward of Woodstock, called the Black Prince, the son and heir of Edward III. He left Bordeaux at the start of October and led his troops for two months, reaching as far as Roussillon. He met the French army in Poitiers on 19 September 1356. The battle ended in a fresh disaster for the Valois, and the king of France, John II (1319-1364), was captured. Amid increasing unrest in Paris, the dauphin, the future Charles V, whose authority was contested, concluded a two-year truce with Edward III in 1357.

Charles of Blois Taken Prisoner, illustration in Froissart's *Chronicles*, around 1410.

In this turbulent context, several rebellions temporarily destabilised France in 1358. At the start of the year, the provost of the merchants of Paris, Étienne Marcel (c. 1316-1358), called the people of Paris to insurrection, whereas in the countryside at Beauvaisis, the peasants, known as Jacques, rose up against the nobility on 28 May, leading to the campaigns in Normandy and Auxerre. These uprisings came to a bloody end shortly after the death of Étienne Marcel on 31 July.

Once the truce between England and France expired in the summer of 1359, Edward III, in a position of strength, raised a new army in Calais. He wanted to reach Reims, where he could be crowned king of France. However, the town put up fierce resistance and the English King was forced to open negotiations with the dauphin of France.

FOREIGN WARS AND DOMESTIC CRISES IN FRANCE AND ENGLAND

The Treaty of Brétigny and the exportation of the conflict (1360-1369)

On 8 May 1360, while he was still being held prisoner, John II was forced to sign the Treaty of Brétigny, which guaranteed the king of England sovereignty over Calais, Ponthieu, Aquitaine, Gascony, Quercy, Limousin and Agenais, or almost a third of the kingdom, in exchange for withdrawing his claim to the French throne. This agreement also set John II's ransom at three million écus, which was equivalent to two years' revenue for the kingdom of France. It was a complete disaster.

This treaty temporarily put an end to the military operations between the two countries, which were ruined by war, disease and famine. The peace was signed in Calais on 24 October 1360. While the decisions taken in Brétigny were ratified by Edward III and John II, the resulting renunciations remained unresolved for a long time. The regions that England had just acquired proved reluctant to submit to their new lords, and many towns closed their doors when English officers arrived. That said, we can consider the territorial clauses to have been applied in 1362. In addition to this reorganisation, France also had to deal with the problem of the King's ransom. John II, who had been released in exchange for hostages, struggled to raise the necessary sum. He died in London before he had paid what he owed, and was succeeded by Charles V. In spite of this treaty, conflict persisted indirectly, notably in Brittany.

A few years later, a new conflict began, with allies intervening in the Castilian succession. Charles V entrusted du Guesclin with the mission of leading the free companies in Spain. Although he was defeated by the Black Prince at the Battle of Najéra in 1367, he nonetheless managed to secure victory for his ally Henry of Trastámara at Montiel in 1369.

After Peter the Cruel refused to pay the amount he had promised in 1367, the following year the Black Prince decided to raise the money to cover this by imposing a new tax on his principality of Aquitaine. John I of Armagnac (c. 1306-1373) rejected this new tax and appealed against it to the King of France. A number of lords in Gascony followed suit. Charles V heeded the appeal and summoned the Black Prince to Paris in 1369. In response, Edward of Woodstock had the two royal messengers murdered. In spite of the terms of the Treaty of Brétigny, Edward III then took up the title King of France, which had been dropped in 1360. On 30 November 1369, Charles V once again pronounced the confiscation of Guyenne.

The renewal of hostilities in France (1369-1380)

The mounting tensions led to the renewal of hostilities in France. In the meantime, the French army had changed significantly, as Charles V had decided to apply the English model of contracts to his men. In this way, like his enemy, he kept at his disposal a permanent core of around 3000 soldiers, and this number could double during military campaigns. Finally, the king was no longer at the front of his troops, but remained further back in order to ensure their command. Additionally, he relied on carefully chosen military leaders, such as du Guesclin, who was named constable in 1369. Charles V also made sure that he had a network of alliances with Castile and Scotland, and secured the neutrality of Flanders.

In spite of a two-year truce (1375-1377), operations continued, although no major battle took place in this period as each side favoured a war of attrition in order to weaken the other. With the aim of preventing the English from resuming the major chevauchées that had brought them their success, the French strengthened fortifications in towns and did not hesitate to resort to a scorched earth policy, leaving the English with no resources. The French also used new pieces of artillery, such as copper and iron cannons, which complemented the traditional weapons which used a counterweight to launch their missiles.

The fighting therefore resumed with greater intensity, and the situation was particularly difficult for England.

Edward III was too old and incapable of leading his kingdom, while his heir was away waging war in Castile and Aquitaine. The Black Prince died on 8 June 1376, followed by his father on 21 June 1377. The French intended to take advantage of this weakness to continue their conquests. In spite of du Guesclin's reluctance, Charles V made an unsuccessful attempt to take Brittany.

In 1380, both du Guesclin and Charles V died. The two kingdoms were both in a delicate position and fighting ceased, with the English only keeping possession of Calais, Brest, Bordeaux and Bayonne.

The war on hold (1380-1415)

In 1380, both kingdoms were beset by doubt. In spite of the dynamic of victories and the reorganisation of the tax system, France was struggling financially. The new king, Charles VI, was just 12 years old. On the English side, the deaths of the Black Prince and Edward III destabilised the kingdom. The young Richard II (1367-1400), the son of Edward of Woodstock, was only ten when he acceded to the throne in 1377. His uncle, John of Gaunt (1340-1399), acted as regent. He did not intend to let the French take advantage of their territorial reconquest, and tried to raise a new tax in 1381 in order to finance a military campaign. However, the population, worn out by wars and plague, rebelled. Although this uprising did not have the desired effect, it nonetheless reached the capital of the kingdom and forced the young king to take refuge in the Tower of London.

During his reign, Richard II tried to consolidate his domestic power and therefore encouraged peace with France. However, although the fighting stopped of its own accord in 1380, no peace was signed. While the English were fighting in Castile, the French nurtured a series of plans to land in England between 1386 and 1387, to no avail. A truce was finally signed in 1388, followed by another, valid this time until 1426. This last pact was sealed by the return of Brest to France and Richard II's marriage to Isabella of Valois (1389-1409), the daughter of Charles VI.

During this period, the situation in France was deteriorating. Although the years 1380-1390 saw a return to prosperity, Charles VI, who was increasingly plagued by bouts of insanity, was no longer capable of governing and left the kingdom under the domination of the nobles and their disputes. This was how the Armagnac-Burgundian Civil War broke out, following the murder of the King's brother, Louis I, Duke of Orléans (1372-1407), on 23 November 1407 by one of John the Fearless' men. The situation was scarcely any better in England, where Richard II also had to deal with a revolt led by Henry of Bolingbroke (1366-1413). On 26 September 1399, Richard II was forced to abdicate in favour of his enemy, who took the name of Henry IV. However, the new king died in 1413, leaving the throne to Henry V (1387-1422). Henry V was determined to restore order and unity to the kingdom, and saw the war against France as a way to achieve his aims.

THE ARMAGNAC-BURGUNDIAN CIVIL WAR

The Armagnacs and the Burgundians were two major French factions who were in opposition because of their political ideas and their relationship to their English enemy.

Following the murder of Louis I, Duke of Orléans, by John the Fearless, the two parties were due to meet on the bridge at Montereau to open discussions on 10 September 1419. However, during the interview John the Fearless was killed by the Armagnacs, who were supported by the dauphin Charles. Immediately, the new duke of Burgundy, Philip the Good (1396-1467) sided with the English. It was not until 1435, during the Congress of Arras, that the two factions were reconciled, with Burgundy returning to the French side.

THE ENGLISH RECONQUEST

England's stranglehold over France (1415-1420)

In 1415, Henry V organised a landing in Normandy and laid siege to Harfleur. Once the town had been taken, he decided to lead his 15 000 men to Calais to spend the winter there. In order to prevent him from retreating, Charles VI raised troops and sent his men to intercept the king of England's soldiers. The encounter took place at Agincourt on 25 October. Leadership mistakes and the inadequacy of their strategy made this battle a disaster for the French army, which was nonetheless far superior in terms of numbers, with no fewer than 50 000 men. The location chosen for the battle was too narrow and did not allow the French forces to be deployed, as there were too many of them. Furthermore, the French knights once again refused to let the foot soldiers open the fighting, and launched an attack in fields that were muddy from the autumn rain. By the end of the battle, almost 10 000 French soldiers were left dead, including some of the most important nobles in the kingdom, compared with only 1600 on the English side.

The Battle of Agincourt, miniature from *l'Abrégé d'Enguerrand de Monstrelet*, 15th century.

The impact of the Battle of Agincourt was so great that Sigismund, Holy Roman Emperor (1368-1437) intervened in 1416 to try and negotiate a peace between France and England. However, Henry V rejected this request, as he was determined to make the most of his advantage. He once again landed in Normandy in 1418 and took over the duchy. By the spring of 1419, the English had reached the outskirts of Paris. At the same time, Henry V was interfering in the Armagnac-Burgundian Civil War and, in December

1419, signed an agreement with Philip the Good. Burgundy was the most powerful duchy in France, so allying with it boosted England's chances of winning the war.

Backed into a corner, Queen Isabeau of Bavaria was forced to sign the disastrous Treaty of Troyes on 21 April 1420, through which the dauphin was removed from the line of succession and replaced by the king of England, Henry V. To seal this agreement, the English King married the daughter of Charles VI, Catherine of Valois (1401-1437). The King of England entered Paris in December 1420.

Hesitation and confusion (1420-1429)

Henry V continued with his conquest and gathered a large army in Calais. The dauphin Charles resisted and won the Battle of Baugé (22 March 1421) in Maine, thus ensuring the survival of his kingdom of Bourges.

The following year, Henry V and Charles VI both died. As Henry VI (1421-1471), the new king of France and England, was only a few months old, John of Lancaster, 1st Duke of Bedford (1389-1435), was appointed regent and placed in charge of Normandy, Maine, Calais and Paris. On the other side, Charles, the dauphin of France, was leading weakened forces and had little support. However, that did not stop him from claiming the title king of France, thus violating the treaty of 1420.

Military engagements continued somewhat confusedly between the Seine and the Loire. Low numbers of troops and leadership problems prevented any decisive victories.

The Duke of Bedford nonetheless decided to set off for Berry and conquer the territories that were still under the dauphin's control.

THE FRENCH RESURGENCE AND VICTORY

France wakes up (1429-1444)

In 1429, the Duke of Bedford laid siege to Orléans. Although he thought he would be able to take the city quickly, the siege dragged on for several long months, before a young peasant girl named Joan of Arc managed to liberate the city on 29 April 1429. It was now necessary to devise a strategy to make the most of this victory, but those around the king were divided between the idea of going to Normandy or retaking Paris. Charles took Joan of Arc's advice and went to Reims so that he could be crowned king of France in the cathedral on 17 July. Through this symbolic act, he planned to position himself as the legitimate sovereign of the kingdom and thus win the loyalty of his subjects. In response, the Duke of Bedford had Henry VI crowned king of France in Paris in 1431.

John of Arc in Armour at Orléans, painting by Jules Eugène Lenepveu, 1886-1890.

The French continued with their operations and, between 1429 and 1430, recaptured the towns of Laon, Soissons, Senlis and Compiègne from the English and Burgundians. However, they failed to take Paris. Faced with the return of the plague and an economic crisis, and growing unrest among the major figures of the kingdom, the king of France was forced to take a break in his reconquest.

JOAN OF ARC

Joan of Arc was born in 1412 in the village of Domrémy, north-east France. She announced that she had heard the voices of Saint Catherine of Alexandria, Saint Margaret and the Archangel Michael telling her to go to the dauphin Charles to drive the English out of the kingdom. These voices also told her that she would lift the siege outside Orléans and that she should take the dauphin to Reims for his coronation. Joan of Arc's intervention was important because it came when the French side was in a very bad way. She not only guided the king in his strategy of attack, but also restored the motivation of the troops and gave new hope to the French people. This is why the English and their allies were so quick to capture her and sentence her to death. Taken prisoner by the Burgundians at Compiègne in 1430, she was sold to the English, judged to be a witch and burnt at the stake in Rouen on 30 May 1431. Joan of Arc's fame quickly spread all across the West. She became a national heroine in the 19th century, was beatified in 1909, and was canonised and proclaimed one of the patron saints of France in 1920.

Although Charles VII did not have the means to continue military operations, he worked to become closer to the Burgundians. Through the Treaty of Arras in 1435, Philip the Good renounced his alliance with England and rallied behind the king of France, thereby putting an end to almost 30 years of civil war in France.

In England, the advocates of peace lost valuable support when the Duke of Bedford died in 1435. Tensions then increased between Cardinal Henry Beaufort (c. 1374-1447), who was in favour of negotiations with France, and the Duke of Gloucester (1394-1447), who supported the war. However, as military defeats piled up for the English, and Charles VII entered Paris on 12 November 1437, Henry VI, who was now of age, decided to negotiate a truce with Charles VII in 1444.

The English leave France (1444-1453)

Charles VII made good use of this truce to completely reorganise the French military forces. Through an order on 15 May 1445, he laid the foundations of a standing army. It was made up of the large order, a group of 15 and then 20 companies, each of which were under the command of a captain. Each company had 100 lances, each of which were accompanied by a page, a valet, two or three archers and a *coutilier* (a foot soldier armed with a lance and a dagger). Consequently, Charles VII could permanently count on a field cavalry of around 12 000 men, as well as the small order, comprising the garrison army and a light cavalry. In order to complete this force, in 1448 he created the body of *francs-archers*, which unfortunately did not prove to be very effective. Charles VII also developed a powerful artillery, thanks to his engineers the Bureau brothers. During the first half of the 15th century, the artillery was diversified, in particular thanks to lighter pieces that were easier to manoeuvre and transport. It is because of them that Charles VII was able to reconquer towns in Normandy and Gascony so quickly.

With this new army behind him, and with the assurance of the support of the Duke of Brittany, Charles VII broke the truce in 1449 and set out to conquer Normandy. The French launched several attacks in the north, centre and west and soundly defeated an enemy that struggled to react, as England could no longer ensure the regular payment of its men's salaries. The King of France took advantage of this to make a triumphant entrance in Rouen on 10 November 1449. On 15 April 1450, he crushed the army sent by Henry VI to provide support to his artillery in Formigny. The towns in Normandy surrendered and, thanks to its military superiority and a skilful policy of mediation, Normandy returned to the French side less than a year after the start of operations.

The French army then made its way down the valley of the Dordogne in spring 1451, defeating the towns one by one until Bordeaux surrendered on 30 June, followed by Bayonne on 20 August. Nonetheless, the people of Bordeaux refused to submit to the King of France and recalled the English in 1452. Henry VI responded to their demand by sending 3000 men led by John Talbot (c. 1384-1453). Charles VII and his Breton allies launched a counter-attack in 1453 and positioned an army of 8000 men on the banks of the Dordogne, close to the town of Castillon. After the people appealed to him, Talbot went back up the river with 5000 men, and a battle broke out on 17 July. The English were quickly overwhelmed by the firepower of the French, who had 300 bombards. In spite of their attempts, the English troops were crushed in just a few hours. Charles VII, who refused to enter discussions with the towns in Aquitaine that were still resisting, managed to subdue them by force, and laid siege to Bordeaux at the end of July 1453. While the rebellious capital was preparing for a long wait, the town's middle classes surrendered on 19 October, fearing the destructive force of the French artillery.

When Bordeaux surrendered, the king of France was now the master of his entire kingdom, with the exception of Calais. The Hundred Years' War was over.

IMPACT

AN ENDLESS WAR

Although the Hundred Years' War is considered to have ended in 1453 with the surrender of Bordeaux, there was no treaty to recognise the end of the fighting. There were still some skirmishes, in particular on the Île de Ré and in the port of Sandwich in 1457. It was not until the Treaty of Picquigny in 1475 that there was an official truce between the two kingdoms.

In spite of everything, the reason historians have settled on 1453 is because one element unites the period of the Hundred Years' War: the threat posed to the integrity of French territory by the presence of the English on the continent. Although the English still had the enclave of Calais in 1453, France as a territorial unit was no longer threatened. This year therefore marks a turning in the turbulent relations between France and England.

A RECONFIGURATION OF THE SOCIAL AND SPATIAL FABRIC

The consequences of the Hundred Years' War on demographics and the organisation of space in both France and England are significant.

Between 1330 and 1450, the kingdom of France lost around 42% of its population, and England lost around 40%. While this demographic collapse was partly a result of the war, primarily in France where the fighting took place, it was also and above all due to the indirect consequences of the combat: crop destruction, famine and epidemics. Furthermore, the population in the countryside was displaced and moved to the towns in search of protection. This was why the lords tried to repopulate their land at the end of the war, and were consequently forced to grant new benefits to the peasants, who naturally joined the lord who offered them the most.

Nonetheless, the towns were also hit hard by the war. In the face of sieges, the destruction of the suburbs and popular unrest, the urban dynamism which had developed before the conflict was affected, even if the demands of the war led to the setting up of a municipal administration which would endure after 1453. Conversely, English towns benefitted from the diversion of many maritime routes in their favour and experienced slow, regular growth in this period, with the appearance of the first cloth industries.

Social relationships were another victim of this climate of constant conflict. Several generations went their entire lives without experiencing peace, which rendered violence somewhat commonplace.

POLITICAL REGIMES IN TOTAL OPPOSITION

The Hundred Years' War had an irreversible impact on the political development of the two kingdoms. While France and England were both feudal monarchies in 1337, by 1453 they had nothing in common with regard to their political ideas and organisation.

Towards royal absolutism in France

The king of France acquired almost absolute power over his kingdom. While royal power was being directly threatened by the presence of the English, Charles VII used propaganda to put in place a whole ceremony around the royal personage, making them a directly elected representative of God. In this way, the king of France became a ruler by divine right. By the end of the war, Charles VII was all-powerful: he controlled taxes, which had now become permanent, he was at the head of a powerful army, and he had at his service a collection of officials who had studied law and were spread across the country, in particular with the creation of provincial parliaments.

Compared with him, the French nobility was completely discredited following, in particular, a significant decline in their income and humiliation resulting from military defeats. This was no longer the time for chivalric exploits, but for an efficient and deadly army trained in war. Nonetheless, several large fiefdoms, in particular Brittany and Burgundy, resisted the centralisation of power. Louis XI (1423-1483), who succeeded Charles VII, continued the impetus to direct domination over the territory, which had begun with his father when the English left. Through a policy of protecting his borders, he guaranteed the control of Languedoc and the Duchy of Savoy in 1462. Subduing Burgundy proved to be a more complex matter, but Louis XI managed to defeat Charles the Bold (1433-1477) during the siege of Nancy. In this way, he recovered Burgundy, Picardy, the Boulonnais, Artois and Hainaut. His project continued with the capture of land left behind by René of Anjou (Duke of Anjou and

Count of Provence, 1409-1480) between 1480 and 1482. All that remained was the Duchy of Brittany, the annexation of which was prepared for by the marriage of the new king Charles VIII (1470-1498) to Anne of Brittany (1477-1514). Meanwhile, Bordeaux was placed under close surveillance, with a fort constructed at each of the two farthest ends of the urban area.

The English parliamentary monarchy takes its first steps

While the French monarchy was progressing towards absolutism based on the divine right of kings, its English counterpart was developing in the opposite direction. Parliament and the nobility emerged from the war as the big winners. This can be explained initially by the English tax system, which had differed from the French system since the Magna Carta in 1215. In England, Parliament granted the king the right to raise taxes. Furthermore, in times of war, the king was forced to defer to the demands of the Lords and the Commons if he wanted to carry out his military operations. This gave the two houses a great deal of power.

Like in France, the English monarchy was reflecting on the nature of power, but whereas one moved towards sacralisation, the other moved towards a parliamentary monarchy, even going so far as to allow the Parliament to make laws instead of the king. England's defeat only discredited the monarchy further, and popular rumours accused the king and his advisors of treachery. In August 1453, the king sank into madness, leaving free reign to the ambitions of the great nobles, who ended up clashing in a civil war, the Wars of the Roses (1455-1485).

THE BIRTH OF NATIONS

The Hundred Years' War marks the birth of a national consciousness in both countries. However, this national consciousness took on different forms.

In England, the construction of a national identity preceded the Hundred Years' War. It appeared naturally in the English people, in particular as a result of the country's unusual geography. As England is an island, its population quickly developed a sense of superiority over the outside world, which was only strengthened by its resounding victories at the start of the Hundred Years' War. In addition, Edward III had been able to exploit his military successes with the people through an active propaganda campaign which was continued by his successors, notably the Lancasters, with the circulation of national epics based on the victories of Henry V.

In France, the situation was very different. Indeed, at the start of the war, the French people did not exist as a single entity. In a vast country with somewhat poorly defined borders, regional differences were still very pronounced. The construction of a shared national identity was therefore the result of work done by important figures in the kingdom. Starting when Charles V acceded to the throne, the work of drawing up a theoretical basis for French unity through the exaltation of a glorious national history and the greatness of the country began. The people's adherence to this identity in the making only came about later on, based around the rejection of the English occupiers, who were considered to be responsible for the hardship of this period.

Finally, a national identity could not be built without promoting a language spoken by all the people. In this sense, the Hundred Years' War marked a major linguistic rupture. In the 1330s, Latin was the language used in official and literary texts, whereas French was the language of the aristocracy and diplomacy on both sides of the Channel. The people, meanwhile, used a range of local dialects. Although he had French heritage, from the start of the war Edward III ordered all his subjects to learn and speak English, and, from 1362 onwards, all trials were conducted in English. All the same, French continued to be used. The real rupture took place under the Lancastrian dynasty. At the turn of the 15th century, the first literary works in English appeared, and its use spread as far as the official acts of the kingdom. Thus, by the end of the Hundred Years' War, French had practically disappeared from England.

In France, efforts were also made to spread the use of French so that it would replace Latin. Charles V therefore endeavoured to promote this national language in all official acts, with the goal of demonstrating the unity and independence of the kingdom. However, it is still necessary to put the popular usage of French into perspective compared with regional languages.

At the end of the Hundred Years' War, then, the two countries faced two very different futures. The war had allowed each of them to form a territorial unit for themselves and to assert themselves as a nation, in this way opening a new phase in the history of Western Europe.

SUMMARY

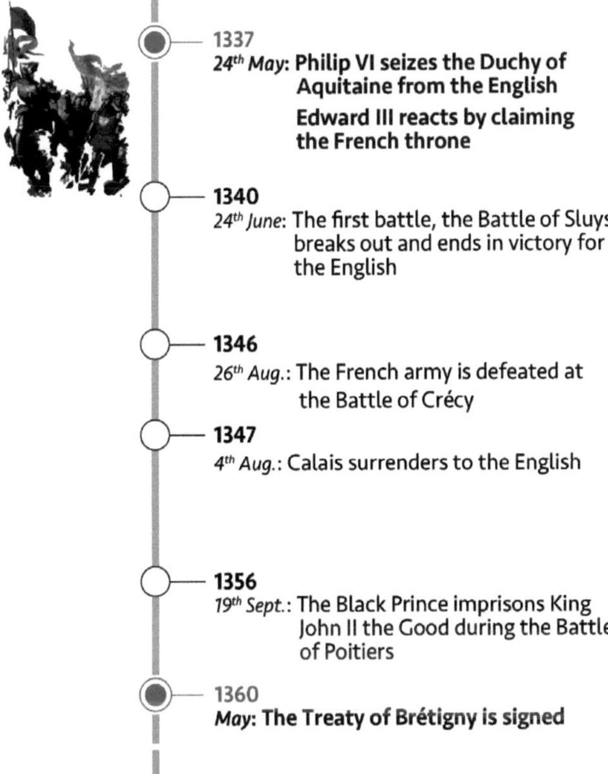

1337

24th May: **Philip VI seizes the Duchy of Aquitaine from the English**

Edward III reacts by claiming the French throne

1340

24th June: The first battle, the Battle of Sluys, breaks out and ends in victory for the English

1346

26th Aug.: The French army is defeated at the Battle of Crécy

1347

4th Aug.: Calais surrenders to the English

1356

19th Sept.: The Black Prince imprisons King John II the Good during the Battle of Poitiers

1360

May: **The Treaty of Brétigny is signed**

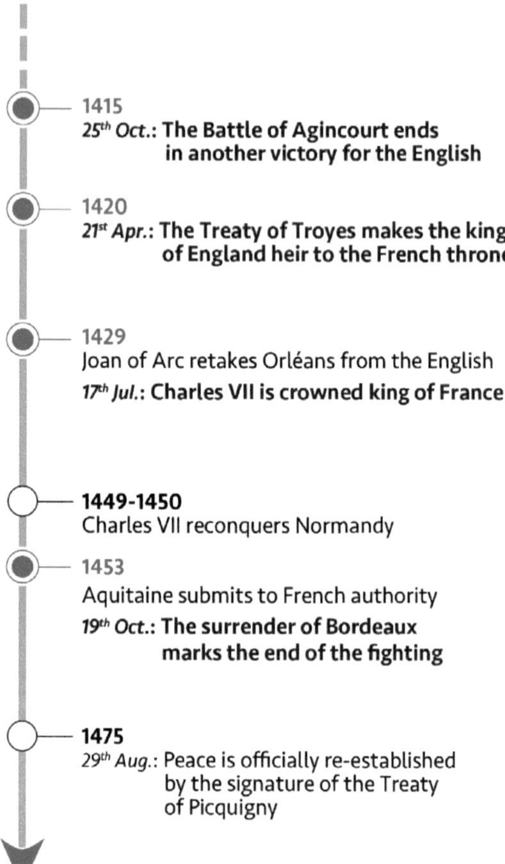

- On 1 February 1328, the king of France Charles IV died without a male heir. His cousin Philip of Valois was named as his successor.

- On 24 May 1337, while the kingdoms of France and England were fighting to ensure hegemony in Flanders, the king of France Philip VI seized the Duchy of Aquitaine from the English. Edward III responded by claiming the French crown.
- In 1340, the Battle of Sluys, the first battle of the Hundred Years' War, took place and was won by the English.
- England won a string of victories in 1346, in particular thanks to the tactic of the chevauchée. In this way, the French army was defeated at Crécy on 26 August, while Calais surrendered to the English on 4 August of the following year.
- In 1356, the two armies met at Poitiers, where King John II was taken prisoner by the Black Prince.
- While he was still a captive, John II was forced to sign the Treaty of Brétigny in May 1360. This meant that he lost a quarter of his kingdom. Nonetheless, Edward III promised to withdraw his claims to the French throne.
- Between 1369 and 1380, King Charles V of France managed to reconquer all the territory lost in the Treaty of Brétigny. The English now only had Calais and Aquitaine.
- Starting in 1388, a series of truces were signed.
- During this period, France was in the grip of the 28-year-long Armagnac-Burgundian Civil War.
- In 1415, the king of England Henry V landed in Normandy and destroyed the French army at Agincourt on 25 October.
- Through the Treaty of Troyes on 21 April 1420, Charles VI recognised the king of England as the heir to the kingdom of France.
- When France was at a very low point, Joan of Arc, driven

by divine voices, entered the war and liberated the town of Orléans in the name of King Charles VII in 1429. She then led the dauphin to Reims so that he could be crowned king.

- Through the Treaty of Arras, signed on 21 September 1435, the Duke of Burgundy Philip the Good sided with France, thus putting an end to the civil war.
- Between 1449 and 1450, Charles VII managed to reconquer Normandy.
- In 1451, the king of France embarked on the conquest of Aquitaine. In spite of fierce resistance, he conquered the province in 1453 following the surrender of Bordeaux on 19 October.
- At the end of the war, Charles VII, who held almost absolute power through the divine right of kings, ruled over all of his territory, which he controlled using his army and his administrative network. Meanwhile, Henry IV, caught in the upheaval of the defeat, was forced to come to terms with a strong Parliament.

BIBLIOGRAPHY

- Autrand, F. (1994) *Charles V le sage*. Paris: Fayard.
- Berland, F. (2013) *Guerre et société. 1270-1480*. Paris: Atlande.
- Bordonove, G. (2006) *Charles VII le Victorieux*. Paris: Pygmalion.
- Butaud, G. (2012) *Les Compagnies de routiers en France (1357-1393)*. Clermont-Ferrand: Lemme Edit.
- Cassagne-Brouquet, S. (2000) *Histoire de l'Angleterre médiévale*. Paris: Ophrys.
- Charmasson, T. (1998) *Chronologie de la France médiévale*. Paris: Presses universitaires de France.
- Contamine, P. (1986) *War in the Middle Ages*. Trans. Jones, M. Oxford: Blackwell Publishing.
- Favier, J. (1980) *La guerre de Cent Ans*. Paris: Fayard.
- Gauvard, C. (2002) *La France au Moyen Âge du Ve au XVe siècle*. Paris: Presses universitaires de France.
- Gauvard, C., De Libera, A. and Zink, M. (2002) *Dictionnaire du Moyen Âge*. Paris: Presses universitaires de France.
- Minois, G. (1993) *Du Guesclin*. Paris: Fayard.
- Minois, G. (2008) *La guerre de Cent Ans : naissance de deux nations*. Paris: Perrin.
- Mollat du Jourdin, M. (1977) *Genèse médiévale de la France moderne*. Paris: Seuil.
- Mollat du Jourdin, M. (1992) *La guerre de Cent Ans par ceux qui l'ont vécue*. Paris: Seuil.
- Paladilhe, D. (2002) *La bataille d'Azincourt 1415*. Paris:

Perrin.
- Sumption, J. (1990) *The Hundred Years War Volume I: Trial by Battle.* Philadelphia: University of Pennsylvania Press.
- Troplong, E. (2000) *De la fidélité des Gascons aux Anglais.* Pau: Princeps Negre Editor.

ADDITIONAL SOURCES

- Barber, R. (1997) *The Life and Campaigns of the Black Prince.* Woodbridge: The Boydell Press.
- Castor, H. (2015) *Joan of Arc.* London: Faber and Faber Ltd.
- Curry, A. and Hugues, M. (1994) *Arms, Armies and Fortifications in the Hundred Years War.* Woodbridge: The Boydell Press.
- Green, D. (2015) *The Hundred Years War: A People's History.* New Haven, Connecticut: Yale University Press.
- Hoskins, P. (2011) *In the Steps of the Black Prince: The Road to Poitiers, 1355-1356.* Woodbridge: The Boydell Press.
- Hoskins, P. and Barber, R. (2016) *Crécy 1346: A Tourists' Guide.* Barnsley: Pen and Sword.
- Jones, M. (2005) *Agincourt 1415: A Battlefield Guide.* Barnsley: Leo Cooper Ltd.
- Jones, M. (2016) *24 Hours at Agincourt.* London: Penguin.
- Nicolle, D. (2000) *Crecy 1346: Triumph of the Longbow.* Oxford: Osprey Publishing.
- Nicolle, D. (2000) *French Armies of the Hundred Years War.* Oxford: Osprey Publishing.
- Sumption, J. (2001) *The Hundred Years War Volume II: Trial By Fire.* Philadelphia: University of Philadelphia

Press.

- Sumption, J. (2012) *The Hundred Years War Volume III: Divided Houses*. London: Faber and Faber Ltd.
- Sumption, J. (2016) *The Hundred Years War Volume IV: Cursed Kings*. London: Faber and Faber Ltd.

ICONOGRAPHIC SOURCES

- *The Battle of Crécy*, illustration from the *Chronicles* of Jean Froissart, 15th century. Royalty-free reproduction picture.
- *Death of Bertrand du Guesclin at the Siege of Randon*, illustration in a manuscript by Jean de Wavrin, 15th century. Royalty-free reproduction picture.
- *Joan of Arc in Reims During the Coronation of Charles VII*, painting by Jules Eugène Lenepveu, 1886. Royalty-free reproduction picture.
- *The Battle of Crécy*, an illustration in *Les Grandes Chroniques de France*, around 1415. Royalty-free reproduction picture.
- *Charles of Blois Taken Prisoner*, illustration in Froissart's *Chronicles*, around 1410. Royalty-free reproduction picture.
- *The Battle of Agincourt*, miniature from *l'Abrégé d'Enguerrand de Monstrelet*, 15th century. Royalty-free reproduction picture.
- *John of Arc in Armour at Orléans*, painting by Jules Eugène Lenepveu, 1886-1890. Royalty-free reproduction picture.

CHRONICLES

- Chandos, J. (2013) *Life of the Black Prince: By the Herald of Sir John Chandos*. CreateSpace Independent Publishing Platform.
- De Monstrelet, E. (2010) *The Chronicles of Enguerrand de Monstrelet*. Charleston, South Carolina: Nabu Press.
- Froissart, J. (1978) *Chronicles*. Trans. Brereton, G. London: Penguin.
- Le Bel, J. (2015) *The True Chronicles of Jean le Bel, 1290-1360*. Trans. Bryant, L. Woodbridge: The Boydell Press.

LITERARY ADAPTATIONS

- Shakespeare, W. (2000) *Henry V*. Ware, Hertfordshire: Wordsworth Editions.
- Shakespeare, W. (2012) *Henry VI, Parts I, II and III*. Basingstoke: Palgrave Macmillan.
- Shakespeare, W. (2013) *Henry IV Parts 1 and 2*. Ware, Hertfordshire: Wordsworth Editions.
- Shakespeare, W. (2013) *Richard II*. Ware, Hertfordshire: Wordsworth Editions.
- Shakespeare, W. (2015) *Richard III*. Ware, Hertfordshire: Wordsworth Editions.

IMPROVE YOUR GENERAL KNOWLEDGE

IN A BLINK OF AN EYE !

www.50minutes.com